Introduction to Structured Analytical Techniques for National Security Analysts: Tradecraft Coursework and Table Top Exercises

Volume 1

First Edition

Editors

C. M. Kelshall & Asha Khera

SFU

LIBRARY

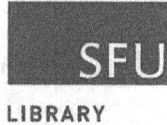

First published in 2018

by Simon Fraser University Library and Canadian Association for Security and Intelligence Studies Vancouver

8888 University Drive, Burnaby, BC V5A 1S6

ISBN 978-1-77287-055-8

CASIS~VANCOUVER~ACERS

SAPERE AUDE

Table of contents:

Chapter 1 - Critical Thinking   1
    by C M Kelshall

Chapter 2 - Key Assumption Check   31
    by Anika Kale & Davina Shanti

Chapter 3 - Quality of Information Check   43
    by Sarah Meyers & Greg Vlassopoulos

Chapter 4 - Indicators and Signposts of Change   57
    by Natalie Archutowski, Marco Autelitano, &
    Emma Curtis

Chapter 5 - Analysis of Competing Hypothesis   67
    by Caitlin Manz & Asha Khera

Chapter 6 - Cross Impact Matrix   81
    by Evan Pearce & Rob van den Boom

Blank Templates   91

References   99

Chapter 2. Media Pack   103

Chapter 3. Media Pack   109

Chapter 4. Media Pack   115

Chapter 5. Media Pack   125

Chapter 6. Media Pack   132

Acknowledgements

Special thanks to Serge Bergler, Rob van den Boom, and Peter Rautenbach for design and formatting. Additional thanks to Natalie Archutowski for the cover design.

Candyce would like to thank Dr. Rihab Elzein and Gail Kelshall for their unfailing patience. To my girls: Chloe Rose Kelshall-Bynoe, Kennedy and Cassidy Kelshall and Jawaher Sanchez Elzein ...*Follow the path*.

Asha would like to thank Rosey and James Donnelly, and Akash Khera for their support.

Editors

Candyce M. Kelshall A former Independent Police Advisor to the British Transport Police and the UK Metropolitan Police. She is the President of the Canadian Association for Security and intelligence Studies in Vancouver, Canada where she is also an Adjunct Professor at Simon Fraser University's School of Criminology. She is a former Royal Navy Reserve Officer and an SCC Officer.

Asha Khera specializes in the study and research of International Relations at Simon Fraser University. She currently manages the Direct Action International dataset at the Centre for 5th Generation Warfare Studies. Asha is also the Executive Officer at CASIS Vancouver and has commanded training exercises in Structural Analytical Techniques as well as overseeing all operations planning within CASIS. She is currently working on her second book, "Terrorism, Identitarians, and Culture Wars," which she is co-authoring with Candyce Kelshall.

Introduction

Critical thinking is the most important tool available to an analyst. The ability to be objective when assessing information requires both art and scientific application. The purpose of this volume is to assist new analysts and researchers with a series of table top exercises to assist with the practice and development of analytical expertise. This book adapts Randolph H. Pherson's and Richards J. Heuer's Structured Analytical Techniques (SATs) as the basis for its exercises, along with complete media packs to be used as a means to update overall analytical and critical thinking abilities.

Chapter 1. Critical Thinking
C M Kelshall

Introduction

Critical thinking is the most important tool available to an analyst. The ability to be objective when assessing information requires both art and scientific application. The purpose of this volume is to assist new analysts and researchers with a series of table top exercises to assist with the drilling and development of analytical expertise.

The exercises included in this volume are all diagnostic in nature and the second edition follows with additional techniques and exercises to enable new analysts to appreciate the need for multiple structured analytical techniques when approaching complex and often contradictory information relating to solving security problems.

Methodology

Solving security problems requires an analyst to approach datasets with a clear idea of the nature of the problem. Selecting the most effective approach to collecting data and determining which data might reveal the most possible, plausible and credible information is the main function of the methodology statement which should precede the application of analytical techniques to a security problem. Designing an appropriate research plan or methodological approach is critical in ensuring that the right information is being sought, in the right manner and applied to the problem in the right way to generate a likely answer to the security enquiry. Methodologies may change by necessity, as more information reveals different paths which need to be investigated.

Critical thinking

The DDEA approach to critical thinking helps to determine, examine, and assess the nature of the subject or question being investigated. The approach, though apparently simplistic, allows the analyst to step away from accepted ideas, perceptions and assumptions based on conventional wisdom and understandings of an issue. We often take information for granted without questioning where the knowledge came from or how we arrived at our acceptance of the meaning we give to things. The DDEA process is a methodical exercise in disassociating accepted knowledge from objective facts as an issue relates to a security problem.

The first four steps in the critical thinking process require you to define, describe, explain, and analyze (DDEA) the key components of the security problem. Defining a problem is often confused with describing the problem. Making the distinction between these two is the first step in addressing a security problem.

Define

Definitions are important. They establish the framework within which information can be interrogated and a value placed on the utility of the object, theory, or occurrence being examined. The role and purpose of defining something is in establishing its reason for existence.

By **Role** we mean:

- What is its function?
- What does it do?

By **Purpose** we mean:

- Why is it necessary?
- Why do we need it?

If we take as an example defining 'methodology':

Role of methodology:

Shapes the approach taken and methods used to collect and collate information in order to arrive at a likely answer to a security problem or study.

Purpose of methodology:

To help you analyse your data collection techniques in order to judge the soundness of the conclusions generated.

Defining an object or occurrence helps to mark the functionality of an object, theory, or occurrence in relation

4

to what is being examined. We might evaluate something based on how well it fulfils its role and purpose. It does it very well, not well, sufficiently, or more information is needed to assess the subject. This is important as a definition helps to provide a unit of measure.

Describe

Describing the physical characteristics of the object or theory being assessed.

- What does it look like?
- How will you recognise it?

A description without a definition (explained above) could lead to confusion. The description when viewed this way is radically different from the role and purpose of an object, a theory or an occurrence.

The description of a methodology would include the steps taken in order to collect information to answer a particular security question. The stages involved might include:

- Determining the research problem
- Formulating the research problem
- Planning the steps of the research study conceptualising the research design
- Data collection determination
- Formulating the research proposal

- Collecting data
- Processing, analysing, and graphically displaying data
- Completing the research report

Explain

To explain means saying how something works:

- Giving the technical specifications of how the object or theory functions or how an occurrence unfolded.
- Indicating the positives and negatives (the good and the bad).
- Indicating how many angles it might be viewed from.

If we take as an example explaining 'methodology':

Discuss the means, procedures, methods and techniques that were used for the collection of your primary data. Explaining, in this context, means divulging detailed information to clarify and rationalise why particular approaches were taken and how those approaches worked. Explaining is distinct from describing. Explaining how a watch might work means discussing how springs move the arms along a watch face in order to keep time.

Analyse

Analysing an issue means applying **reasoned judgement** to the evidence collected, in order to make a determination or statement about the security question or problem. Using the DDEA approach helps in ensuring a conclusion is sound and the correct approaches are used in answering the question.

Reasoned judgement might be best defined as informed opinion which is substantiated by supporting evidence which is plausible (reasonable), verifiable (accurate or justified) and credible (believable or possible). The opinion resulting might be considered an informed assessment of available information, if it is based on a DDEA approach.

If we use the following example as practice of analysis:

1. Look at a to-go coffee mug. Place the mug in front of you and write what you see from your single point of view.
2. Now turn the mug around, record what you see from that point of view.
3. Compare your notes, were each of the sides viewed differently? Usually, they are. This is called perception and when you analyze material perception matters. Therefore, it is important to self-reflect during analysis and ensure you are looking at all possible outcomes or take the

initiative to introduce as many possible perceptions as may be relevant to an issue.

To this end, criticism, limitations, parameters are also important.

Criticism of something occurs when the object, theory or occurrence does not conform to its definitions.

Limitations occur when the object, theory or occurrence does conform to its definition but in some circumstances or contexts performs less than adequately according to its definition or role and purpose.

Parameters are the contexts within which something is being analysed. It might be geographical, time-based, theme-spaced or demographic.

Following the process of DDEA, you are now ready to construct your position (hypothesis) and arguments in order to make an enquiry into the security problem. Keep in mind: your argument and position should always be based around defending, countering or dismissing a logical and reasoned stance on a subject, object, theory, or occurrence.

Hypothesis

A hypothesis is a supposition which is asserted on the basis of some known facts, which is a starting position for an enquiry.

A hypothesis describes what you expect to find as a result of your research. It is a statement, not a question, and therefore a narrow, specific statement(s) of prediction.

There are two forms of hypotheses: null and alternative

Null hypothesis: makes a prediction that no relationship exists between groups on a variable. The aim is to support the prediction or prove it wrong.

Alternative hypothesis: a directional hypothesis which make a prediction about the expected outcome. Moreover, they include non-directional hypotheses which anticipate a difference but do not state what kind of difference. A prediction is based on a best guess or forecast.

If we take examples of null and alternative hypotheses:

Null Hypothesis: there is no difference or relationship between (the classes being examined)

Alternative Hypothesis; directional: scores will be higher for Class A than Class B

Alternative Hypothesis; non-directional: there is a difference between Class A and Class B

Arguments

An **argument** is the presentation of reasons and evidence in support of an idea, that is to say, the means by which a position is proven.

Why do we need arguments?

The purpose of an argument is to justify a position taken, ensuring that evidence is used to prove that the argument is valid. The use of evidence in arguments is crucial to avoiding common analytical pitfalls such as anchoring and cognitive bias. Evidence must be collected which both disproves and proves a position, in order to judge the rigour of the position.

When do we use arguments?

Arguments are used to:

- Support a position or point of view
- Persuade someone into a particular course of action
- Convince someone that something is true or likely to be true
- Demonstrate the problems or difficulties with an approach

How are arguments formed?

Arguments provide a portfolio of proof regarding a position taken on a question, subject, or object.

The use of an argument reduces as much as possible the bias of perception. This is valid and only follows when the analyst presents counter-arguments based on others' perceptions. An argument is comprised of both claims and grounds.

Claims to an argument can be either prescriptive or descriptive.

Descriptive claims are either designative (factual) or definitive (how do we define or categorise something? What is it?)

Prescriptive claims are either evaluative (value judgements) or advocative (lobby for a particular position to be taken)

Grounds might be described as the basis upon which a claim is being made. It might also be considered the evidence used to support a claim, without grounds a claim is an opinion.

There are two categories of grounds, acceptable or unacceptable.

Acceptable grounds can be quotes, historical facts, published experts, or empirical evidence from reliable sources.

Unacceptable grounds can include outdated data, non-academic (unsourced) non- verified and non- credible sources, personal life experiences, and personal opinion.

Position

A position statement made to facilitate an enquiry into a security problem is effectively a hypothesis.

The position is defended by presenting arguments which are supported by credible evidence associated with the argument.

An argument needs to have a position that it is defending. Without a position the argument is only a statement. Further, a position is only as strong as the arguments that support it.

Evidence

Evidence is used within your argument to support the position. However, evidence should be obtained to disprove a hypothesis as well. It is particularly important to assess the veracity, probability, and credibility of evidence.

The collection of evidence includes referencing primary sources or data sets. Primary sources and data sets are key to making an analysis based on your specific security problem. Secondary academic sources are reports or published datasets or assessments which have been previously analyzed based on evidence being selected to answer another security question, or to address a different security problem. For this purpose, previously published material may not be relied upon unless there is a clear indication of methodology, design, choice of approach and data collection methods. Previously published secondary sources including reputable and credible sources have all been written and researched for specific agendas or to fulfil specific mandates or answer specific questions which may or may not yield access to the immediate security problem's context or requirements.

Single Sourcing

In the field, in the domain of operations or in the battlespace, the use of a single source is not recommended. A single source, especially a source from the perspective of a cultural outsider, places perceptions on evidence which may not be a correct assessment of the local motivation or cultural influence, when in the field. In the operational theatre, where local primary sources of information are more easily obtained, it is recommended that the most recent and up to date information be checked across second or third-party assessment. Relying solely on single sourced information which may be dated or created without a significant and nuanced understanding of cultural context is not recommended.

Your evidence should be designed to address the veracity, probability, and credibility of evidence, this ensures a higher degree of confidence in the finished product.

Drawing conclusions

A conclusion is the judgement, decision, or opinion formed after an investigation or thought process (DDEA) using the available facts. A conclusion states the outcome and presents the justification for the outcome.

Conclusions make connections using background knowledge, predictions, and the evaluation of facts.

Emotional Bias

Avoid being emotionally tied to one belief, opinion, or assumption and the use of emotional language. Conclusions that are based on emotions rather than an emphasis on facts or discovered information are flawed.

Commit to the facts, let the evidence lead you rather than choosing evidence that fits what you want the outcome to be. The conclusion is in place to reiterate the answer or best assessment based on the position adopted, and therefore to justify the outcomes presented in context and process. Positions can also be disproven by the available information. In such circumstances emotional allegiance to the initial position is counter productive. The first effort in investigation should always be to disprove a position before determining that it is possibly or likely valid.

The briefing note

Briefing notes are used to keep decision and policy makers informed about specific security issues. Briefing notes are the principal means of communication between analysts and decision makers.

Characteristics of a briefing note:

A quality briefing note can efficiently and quickly inform a decision maker on a security issue. For this to occur briefing notes should be:

Short*:* one to two pages and less than 1000 words

Concise: briefing notes should use the BLUF format (explained below)

Reliable: the information used in a briefing note should be credible, accurate and current.

Readable: briefing notes should use plain language and clear headings to make reading easier.

A good BN must be able to distil complex information into a short, well-structured document. Although it is a general briefing statement, it is intended that recommendations and options are included. Justification for choice of recommendation must be presented. This should take the form of a counter approach and reasons why this may be less desirable. For this reason, your BN must have a clear position, clear arguments, and clear evidence for the position being taken.

The structure expected is as follows:

1. Purpose statement: Why this is an issue. This is the answer to the security question you are posing and explain why your security question is relevant.
2. Problem statement: What is the problem and to whom, caused by whom or what. This should give your reader the setting for your analysis by providing the context by giving circumstances or facts regarding your issue. What is the problem and to whom, caused by whom, or what.
3. Summary of key facts: What has occurred and from which perspective.
4. Background: Supply the reader with the information that is essential to understanding the security problem.
5. Key considerations: Implications and for whom – specifically.
6. Perspectives: What alternative perspectives are there? Which other views might we consider on the other side of this issue or affecting other aspects of the problem.
7. What is not known: What must recommendations take into account.
8. Next steps.

Questions to consider:

1. Why you are writing the BN (your purpose).
2. Who you are writing the BN for (your reader/customer).
3. What that person most needs to know.
4. What points you will cover.
5. How you will structure your information.

BLUF format intelligence writing style

Adapted from University of Texas.

Bottom Line Up Front (BLUF): In the BLUF format, the first sentence of each paragraph will sum up all of the information in the paragraph. Therefore, allowing decision makers to quickly skim intelligence products without sacrificing clarity.

A good BLUF should cover all of the information in a paragraph, like an umbrella.

If the paragraph contains any information that doesn't fall under the BLUF's "umbrella," statement for that paragraph that information should be moved to a more appropriate paragraph or the BLUF should be changed to include the additional information.

The component sentences in the paragraph should be arranged from most to least important. This ensures that readers are immediately aware of your product's most important points and that readers can locate information easily.

It is most effective to get right to the point, which is why BLUF is the best way for intelligence analysts to communicate with policymakers and commanders, who are often too busy to read and carefully digest every word of the intelligence products they rely upon to make decisions.

Title: The title of an intelligence product should function as "the ultimate BLUF" in your product. The title – which should succinctly represent the contents of the product – should be thought of as a contract between you and your reader, in that you promise to provide the reader with no more and no less information than the title conveys. Creating an accurate title is extremely important.

Title, Introduction, and Executive Summary: Your title, introduction, and executive summary will usually be the last part of your product that is written, because each of these components must summarize everything contained in the product.

The Problem Statement (Context and Parameters): Use this section to provide the reader with the context of your analysis but be careful not to confuse context with background. The context section should give your reader a setting for your analysis by providing additional information about the set of circumstances or facts regarding the issue you've analysed, while the background section should supply the reader with information that is essential to understanding the issue.

Key Considerations/Implications: The section that follows the background section will contain your analysis and will generally be the longest part of the paper.

When communicating your analysis, it is imperative that you communicate in a way that is accurate, brief and clear

Writing clear and concise products forces analysts to carefully order their thoughts and think critically, and prevents accidental or intentional misrepresentation of the facts, thus improving the final analytical product.

There is no place for the analyst's opinion or editorializing in intelligence analysis. Everything that you write must be based on facts that have been analysed logically and, as much as possible, without biases.

Template for preparing briefing notes

MEMORANDUM for:

Date:

(For Decision)

SUMMARY OF BN IN TOTAL (EXECUTIVE SUMMARY):
Use BLUF guidelines.

POSITION OR PURPOSE STATEMENT
This provides an overview of why the BN is required. It defines (role and purpose) any actions that need to be taken to address a security problem.

THE SECURITY PROBLEM
The security problem must be clearly defined.

(Ex If there was a riot what was the role and purpose or intention of the riot. In this way we distinguish between describing acts or actions which occurred (the immediate cause) and defining the act. What is the immediate cause? Why is this a problem? Who is it a problem to? What are the underlying causes which are expressed in the form of the immediate cause, immediate actions or immediate events?)

BACKGROUND AND KEY FACTS
A brief summary of the background, how we came to need this BN. Good Background presents two perspectives that of the referent object and subject

20

KEY CONSIDERATIONS AND IMPLICATIONS

They should be concise.

ALTERNATIVE PERSPECTIVES TO BE CONSIDERED

Community impact assessments on the affected community are a good way of representing potential alternative perspectives.

WHAT IS NOT KNOWN

What information is missing or needed?

NEXT STEPS

To obtain required missing information.

AVAILABLE OPTIONS

Consider the following options or sub-options:

RECOMMENDATION AND JUSTIFICATION

Approved / Not Approved

Attachments:

The use of references is required.

GRINTSUMS

Definition: A graphical intelligence summary (GRINTSUM) is a visual representation of a synthesized intelligence product used to convey valuable intelligence to decisionmakers.

A GRINTSUM's purpose is to presuppose any uncertainty and reduce likely risks that could be foreseen by decisionmakers and/or ops commanders. To do this, GRINSTUMs must have certain elements that each play their role in demystifying the fog of war that so often surrounds intelligence analysis. Usually, GRINSTUMs are made with presentation software. It depends on the objective of the mission for which the GRINTSUM is to be used, but usually all GRINTSUMs follow a simple format.

They must have each of the following:

1. State the security question up front and in plain view. This allows the commander to see the overall goal which the mission must support.
2. The overall objectives of the mission should be stated clearly and decisively. This will be the end state and will inform the mission's main effort.
3. A visual depiction of the area of operations, be it a map or floorplan, so that the commander can see a literal picture of his/her team's operational needs, thus unclouding the commander's view.
4. An assessment of the current situation, to brief the commander on events happening on the ground.

Such an assessment further reduces uncertainty and gives the commander adequate information, thus enabling him/her to make decisions based on actionable intelligence, rather than incomplete or inaccurate reporting on the ground.

5. Visually depict the number of committed threats that could potentially harm the overall goal of the mission. This aids the commander's operational intelligence. i.e, where, when, how many forces to send/activate.

6. Evidence should be displayed in a clear and enumerated manner. The GRINTSUM is policy-oriented and must therefore have clearly spelled out reasons for why an action must be taken. Thus, the reason for providing consistent, well researched evidence in the GRINTSUM.

Importance of a GRINTSUM

As with most intelligence products, the GRINTSUM reduces uncertainty and provides clear policy objectives for decisionmakers. The GRINTSUM conveys in a clear and efficient manner what the security problem is, how to work toward answering/solving the problem, what the overall objectives are, and why the mission is important. GRINTSUMs provide a quick overview of a complex issue, thus enabling the commander to act quickly on relatively good intelligence. Therefore, GRINTSUMs are useful in daily intelligence reporting, because they take into account the situation on the ground.

Placemats

GRINTSUMs are not only used in intelligence analysis but also in civilian practice and are called placemats. The general idea of a placemat is the same as a GRINTSUM but in civilian sphere they present unclassified information gathered from open source intelligence (OSINT) and are useful in delivering a 5-minute briefing to business leaders, classrooms, policymakers, and other leaders.

Placemats have all the elements of a GRINTSUM but must not necessarily conform to the rigid standards imposed by a military-style briefing. In placemats, arguments can be made on the basis of reasoned and evidentiary-based opinions, rather than hard and indisputable facts.

Conclusion

The next five chapters will explain different diagnostic structured analytical techniques which are meant to be used in conjunction with Contrarian Techniques and Imaginative Thinking Techniques, both of which can be found in volume 2 of the Structured Analytical Techniques workbook. It is critical that you work through critical thinking, and the briefing note before moving onto the tabletop exercises. A good grasp of GRINTSUMS is also recommended.

Figure 1

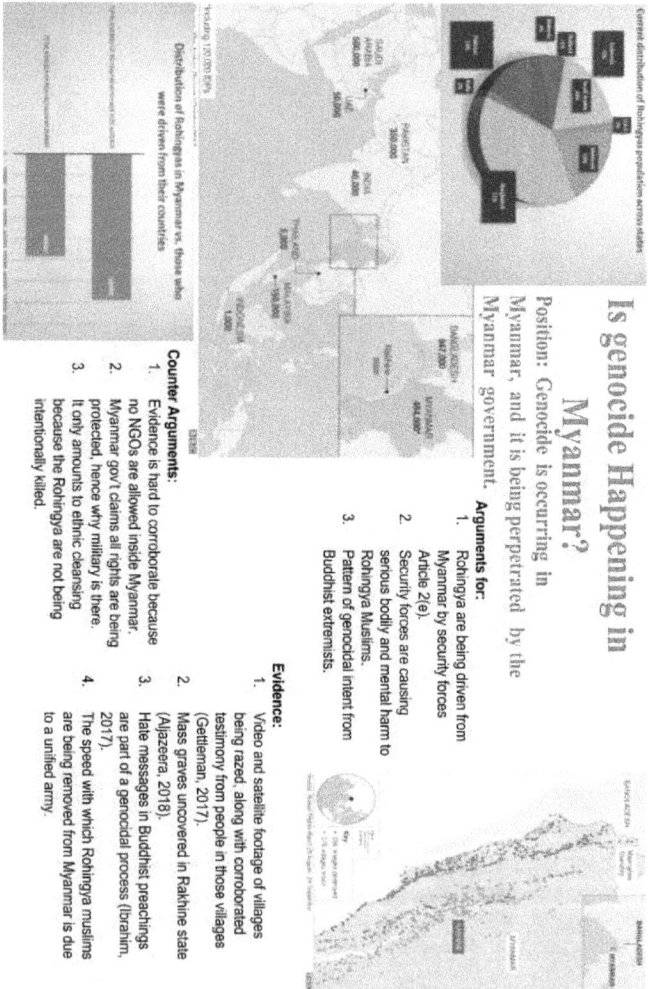

Figure 1. Placemat Example 1. By G. Vlassopoulos, C. Claudel, and M. Chan, 2018. Copyright 2018 by CASIS Vancouver. Reprinted with permission.

Figure 2

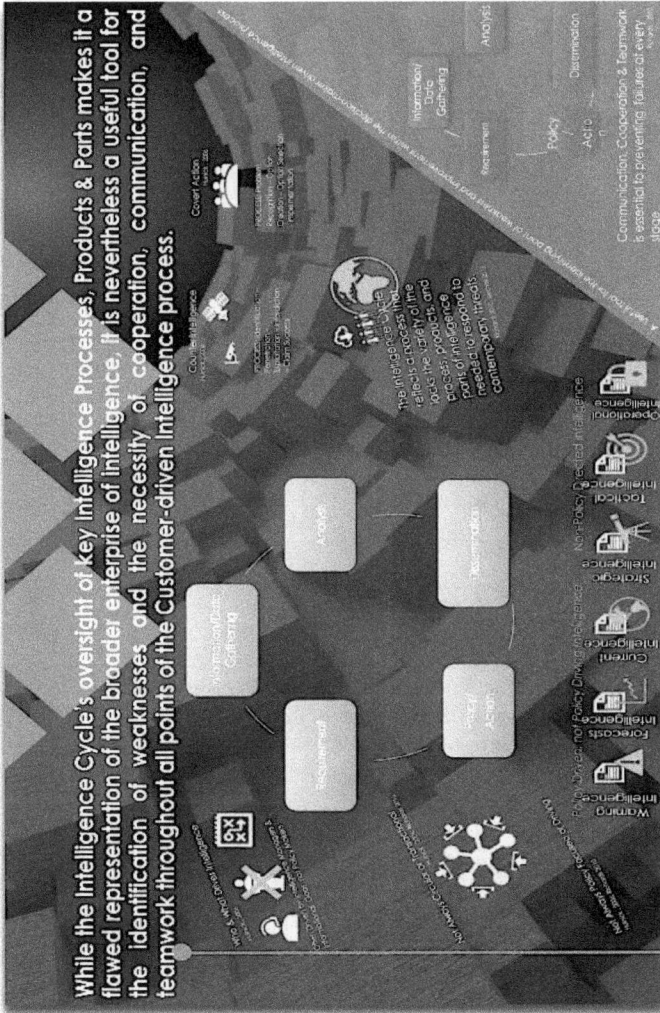

Figure 2. Intelligence Cycle by S. Bergler and V. Dima, 2018.
Copyright 2018 by CASIS Vancouver. Reprinted with permission.

Figure 3

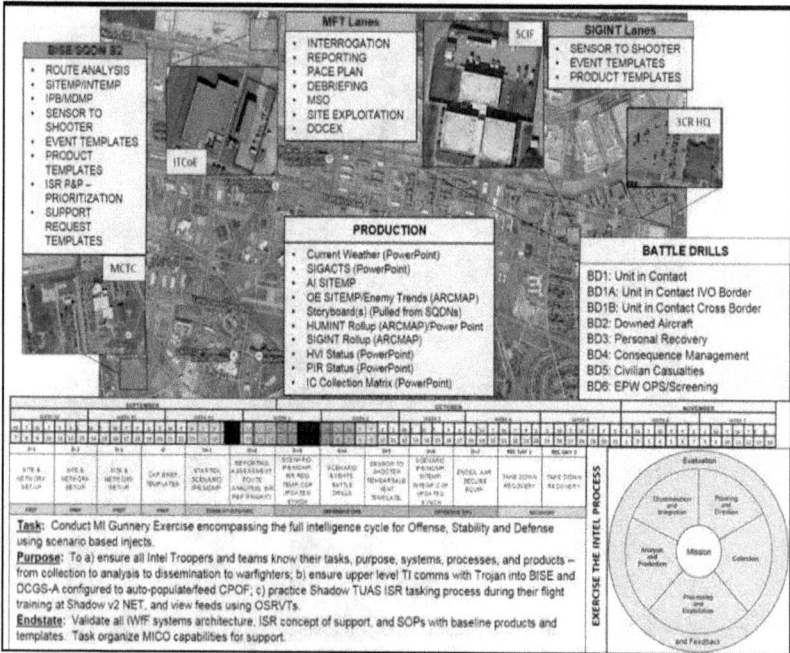

Figure 3. Fundamentals, Adapative Leadership and Mission Command: Meeting the Challenge of Executing Missions in Deployed Environments While Maintaining Home-Station Readiness. Reprinted from *Calvary & Armor Journal*, by K. D. Admiral, B. D. Barker, P. D. Erickson, and D. C. Buchanan, 2017, retrieved from http://www.benning.army.mil/infantry/magazine/issues/2017/ OCT-DEC/PDF/2)Erickson-3rdCR_txt.pdf.

Figure 4

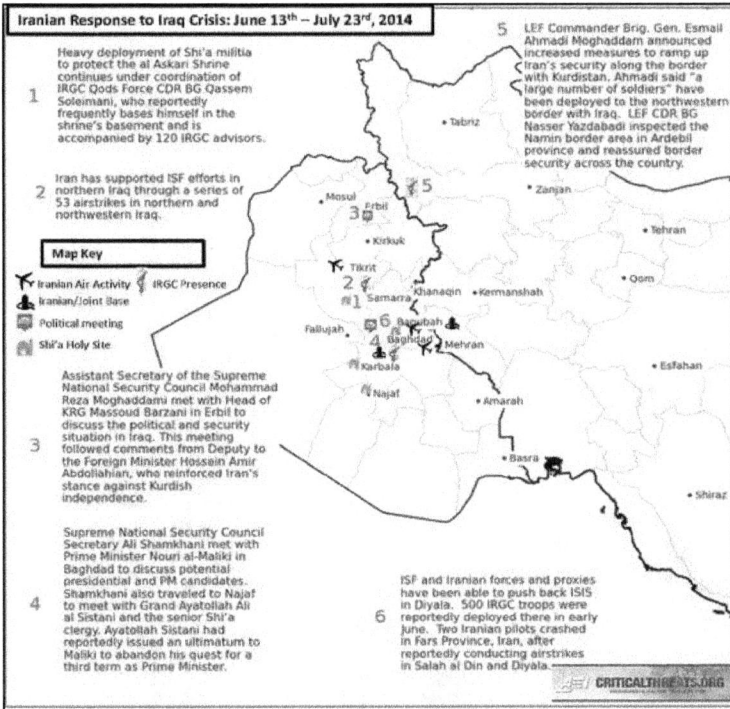

Figure 4. Iranian Response to Regional Crisis: July 23 – August 7, 2014. Reprinted from *Critical Threats*, by M. Moare and F. W. Kagan, August 12 2018, retrieved from https://www.criticalthreats.org/analysis/iranian-response-to-regional-crisis-july-23-august-7-2014

Chapter 2. Key Assumption Check

Anika Kale & Davina Shanti

Tasks

001 - Training objectives

002 - What is a KAC

003 - When to use a KAC

004 - Why use a KAC

005 - How to use a KAC

006 - Steps

006 - Benefits of a KAC

007 - Limitations of a KAC

008 - Example of a KAC table

009 - Table top exercise scenario

010 - Exercise terminology

011 - Exercise context

012 - Competence examination

013 - Candidates analyze sources provided and conduct a
    KAC
014 - Candidates present to panel for competency
    evaluation using GRINTSUM

Training objective

The training objective is to educate candidates on how to use a Key Assumption Check (KAC) in order for candidates to accurately conduct intelligence analysis and therefore prepare them to create reliable intelligence products for decision makers. Candidates will assemble a briefing note on their findings in the form of a GRINTSUM.

What is a KAC

A KAC is a type of diagnostic SAT which limits the presence of bias and flawed judgement in intelligence analysis. It is best to use a KAC at the beginning of intelligence analysis so that analysts are aware of their biases and can fact check them using information. This limits the occurrence of flawed judgement.

When to use a KAC

It is best to use a KAC at the beginning of intelligence analysis so that analysts are aware of their biases and can fact check them using information. This limits the occurrence of flawed judgement.

Why use a KAC

A key assumption check is used to guide an analyst's interpretation of intelligence data and reasoning behind a conclusion. Identifying assumptions can explain the logic behind each assumption and expose cognitive biases. Each analyst may hold assumptions about the security problem which can lead to flawed judgement. Listing and reviewing assumptions at the beginning of the assessment will limit the presence of cognitive biases in the final judgement of the security problem. By limiting the occurrence of cognitive bias, analysts can produce more objective and credible judgements.

How to use a KAC

First, list key assumptions. Key assumptions are any hypothesis an analyst or group accepts to be true. These can be assumptions about a situation, group, or topic. Record all assumptions on a matrix, then examine each assumption by assessing the validity. Ask why the assumption must be true and whether it remains true under all circumstances. Assign each assumption to one of the following categories: *Highly likely, likely,* or *possible*. State why the assumption was categorized that way and record this under the "Assessments" column of the matrix. Refine the list of key assumptions to contain only the assumptions that are true. Consider limitations to the validity of these assumptions. Under what conditions would these assumptions be likely?

What new information could discredit the validity of each assumption?

Steps

1. Team members list assumptions regarding a security problem. All assumptions should be listed in a column of a matrix titled "Assumptions".
2. Team members divide up sources and assess each source for its reliability.
3. The validity of each assumption is assessed using the information from the sources provided.
4. Based on the information, each assumption is categorized as *highly likely, likely*, or *possible*. The categorization of each assumption is listed under a separate column of the matrix titled "Assessment".
5. Once all assumptions are assessed, refine the list to include only the highly likely or true assumptions.
6. Re-examine current assumptions and see if new assumptions need to be added, re-assess assumptions if new information is available.
7. After assessment is complete, key assumption list should only contain those that are true.

Benefits of a KAC

Key assumptions checks can improve intelligence judgements by reducing the frequency and severity of error in assessments and estimates. This SAT aids in limiting the occurrence of cognitive bias when forming a judgement and guides analysts in organizing an abundance of evidence and assessing the validity of each assessment using relevant data. This ensures that the analyst's thought process is more logically sound by improving the accuracy and objectivity of the final judgement.

Limitations of a KAC

Not all assumptions will be recognized. Additionally, hidden assumptions are difficult to assess because they are held unconsciously and are therefore rarely examined or checked for validity. Groupthink is a common cognitive bias that occurs when teams assess key assumptions, therefore all assumptions need to be evaluated thoroughly to avoid biases that may lead to inaccurate judgements. An abundance of information may cause data to become lost or for analysts to neglect information.

Example of a KAC matrix

Assumptions	Assessment
A) Assumption 1	
B) Assumption 2	
C) Assumption 3	
Etc.	

Validity Scale:

Possible	1
Likely	2
Highly Likely	3

Rate each assumption as either *possible, likely*, or *highly likely* based on the assessment given.

CASIS Vancouver

Table top exercise: KAC
Exercise scenario

This chapter's table top exercise security question: *Is there a need for a response to the influence of Soldiers of Odin on alt-right radicalization and possible kinetic activity?*

Exercise terminology

Soldiers of Odin: A right-wing extremist group with the goal of protecting Finnish and Nordic bloodlines.

Alt-right radicalization: The possession of extreme right radical positions on political and social issues.

Kinetic Activity: An action that involves active warfare or force.

Exercise context

Soldiers of Odin are a right-wing extremist group "looking to protect Finnish and Nordic bloodlines" and are known for their anti-immigration stance. They have spread to other countries, and adapt themselves to protect white members of the community they are in. Their influence in communities across Europe has now spread to the United States and Canada.

The group was founded in Kemi, Finland and established as a response to an influx of immigrants arriving in Finland. The group has a history of spreading to other nations such as Canada, Australia, Germany, Sweden, Estonia, the US and the UK. It creates cause for concern as the Soldiers of Odin adapt their chapter's mandates to protect the European ancestry of that nation. For example, in Australia, the Soldiers of Odin adapt to protect Caucasian Australians who are of European descent. The founder, Mika Ranta, has connections with the neo-Nazi Finnish Resistance Movement, and has been convicted of aggravated assault and racially aggravated assault. Soldiers of Odin popularized their presence in 2016 after the sexual assaults on New Year's Eve in Germany and the death of a Lebanese Social worker in Sweden. They establish themselves to be vigilantes who work alongside local law enforcement, but the events such as immigrant-related attacks contradict their mission statement. This changes them from being protectors of European descent to a radicalized group with violent tendencies.

Soldiers of Odin are gaining momentum and expanding across European countries and in Canada. This creates cause for concern as the Soldiers of Odin may influence civilians/local forces and create potential destabilization.

Author adaptations of Google Earth images pinpointing SOO activity, arguably, to spread SOO values and messaging.

Figure 5

Figure 5: SOO activity in Scandinavia (2018)

Figure 6

Figure 6: SOO activity in Northern Europe (2018)

40

Competence examination

By the end of this chapter, candidates should be able to critically think about biases that may hinder an analyst's interpretation of evidence and the reasoning which underlies any particular judgement or conclusion. Candidates should also be able to create a KAC matrix and represent that in the form of a GRINTSUM.

All Media Pack information for analysis can be found in the Media Pack section under Chapter 2.

Chapter 3. Quality of Information Check

Sarah Meyers & Greg Vlassopoulos

Tasks

001 - Training objective

002 - What is a QIC

003 - When to use a QIC

004 - Why use a QIC

005 - How to use a QIC

006 - Benefits of a QIC

007 - Limitations of a QIC

008 - Example of a QIC table

009 - Table top exercise scenario

010 - Exercise terminology

011 - Exercise context

012 - Competence examination

013 - Candidates analyze provided sources and conduct a QIC

014 - Candidates present to panel for competency evaluation using GRINTSUM

Training objective

The training objective is to educate candidates on how to use a quality of information check in order for candidates to accurately conduct intelligence analysis and therefore prepare them to create reliable intelligence products for decision makers.

What is a QIC

A quality of information check is a structured analytical technique used in intelligence analysis to evaluate the "completeness and soundness of available information sources" in order to produce accurate intelligence products for decision makers (US Government, 2009).

When to use a QIC

Establishing the validity of information is essential to creating usable intelligence products for decision-making. Therefore, for any productive analysis and critical thinking to occur, one must first validate the collected information and their sources before moving forward. Specifically, when addressing Open Source Intelligence (OSINT), it is necessary to use a quality of information check to ensure that the information is both quantitatively and qualitatively valid. Once the quality of information of the collected data has been reviewed, it can then be analyzed further, knowing what strengths or weaknesses that the collected information holds. A quality of information check should not be limited to a single use, it is an ongoing process that should occur whenever the understanding of an issue or source changes.

Why use a QIC

The reasoning behind a quality of information check resides in the fact that to create an actionable intelligence product, one must first have valid information to use. A quality of information check allows for a continuous process that provides a confidence level for collected information, which then allows for the intelligence to be analyzed on the basis of the confidence rating as well as what is stated by the source itself. Additionally, a quality of information check allows for intelligence gaps to be easily identified, which in turn can guide intelligence collectors in collecting further information that addresses the identified gaps.

How to use QIC

Following the collection phase of the intelligence cycle, all the collected data on an issue should be analyzed and evaluated based on confidence level. All sources need to be re-evaluated regularly as intelligence gaps are filled and the overall picture of the situation evolves. This is important because the validity of a source may change as new information is uncovered. The confidence rating of collected information, when kept updated, illustrates a clear process for how analysts should approach the information that has been provided, and how they should analyze such data based on emerging information. Overall, the use of a quality of information check is not limited to any distinct portion of the intelligence cycle but should be used whenever new information is passed from intelligence collectors to analysts.

Benefits of a QIC

The most important positive outcome from a quality of information check is the confidence to use a source and the information it provides with a high degree of certainty that it is applicable and valid. When the level of confidence can be clearly measured and compared against other sources, analysts can then create more usable intelligence which allows for more appropriate and well-tailored responses. Additionally, a quality of information check allows for biases and motives to be taken into account, which if not addressed, could easily misdirect analysts. Overall, a quality of information check provides insight for analysts that goes beyond the information provided by the source and illuminates hidden issues that are present due to biases and assumptions created by the source itself. Therefore, this SAT addresses the important issue that information can be misleading if the lens through which it is being observed or presented is not acknowledged and evaluated.

Limitations of a QIC

Similar to other SATs, there are drawbacks to a quality of information check. The first issue is that if an individual does not address and account for their own personal biases, then those same biases presented in an intelligence source could be overlooked. This can also occur on a larger group scale, if the group analyzing the data came from similar backgrounds or share similar beliefs. To counter this issue, individuals of diverse backgrounds and beliefs must analyze and rate intelligence sources to provide possible different confidence rates that can then be compared. Though this does not guarantee that biases and ulterior motives will be recognized, it does help to minimize the possibility of this issue. A second issue that must be acknowledged when using a quality of information check is that the confidence rating system is not a quantitative approach with clear markers to merit a certain rating. Therefore, what one individual may rate a source could be quite different from how another individual may rate the same source. This lack of consistency further highlights the importance of constantly re-evaluating sources as new information emerges and the view of an intelligence problem evolves.

Example of a QIC table

Source	Relevance Level	Confidence Level

Confidence Level (soundness)	Description
A - completely reliable	No doubt regarding authenticity, trustworthiness, integrity, competence. History of complete reliability.

B - usually reliable	Some doubt regarding authenticity or trustworthiness or integrity or competence (one count). History of general reliability.
C - fairly reliable	Doubt regarding authenticity, trustworthiness, integrity, competence (two counts and more). History of periodic reliability.
D - usually not reliable	Definite doubt regarding authenticity, trustworthiness, integrity, competence. History of occasional reliability.
E - unreliable	Certainty about lack of authenticity, trustworthiness, integrity, competence. History of unreliability.
F - undetermined	Cannot be judged (at this time).

Source: *United Nations. (2011). Criminal intelligence: Manual for analysts. United Nation Office on Drugs and Crime.*

Relevance Level (completeness)	Description
5 - very relevant	Addresses security problem. Gives possible answer to security problem.
4 - relevant	Addresses security problem.
3 - somewhat relevant	Addresses aspects of security problem.
2 – not likely relevant	Mentions aspect of security problem without relevant context.
1 - irrelevant	Does not address any aspect of security problem
0 - undetermined	Cannot be judged (at this time).

Table top exercise: QIC
Exercise scenario

The security question that will be addressed in candidates' QIC is the following: Does the threat posed by Daesh in Iraq require more kinetic involvement from the Canadian Armed Forces (CAF) through Operation: Impact?

Exercise terminology

Operation: Impact: is the Canadian Armed Forces contribution to the coalition against Daesh. This initiative began in 2014, with Canada contributing aircraft and special forces advisors to the global coalition. As of 2016, the involvement of Canadian aircraft in airstrikes was halted, but the number of military advisors and trainers were greatly increased as Canada shifted to a more supporting role in the fight against Daesh.

Daesh: also known as the Islamic State of Iraq and Syria (ISIS), is a United Nations recognized terrorist organization, whose area of influence is primarily situated in Western Iraq and Eastern Syria. The group's fundamentalist ideology is based upon the Salafi doctrine of Sunni Islam, which has translated into the group carrying out serious human rights abuses and war crimes in the states of Iraq and Syria. In response to these acts, a coalition of 79 states has created a global initiative to eliminate Daesh and return control to the state governments of the affected regions.

Kinetic Warfare: is the use of military force against another state or group. This process is considered the more classical method of waging war, as it uses lethal force to achieve the desired result, which has been done for thousands of years. An example of such a process can be demonstrated by the United States' invasion of Iraq in 2003, and how the use of kinetic warfare was the primary method that the American government implemented to remove Saddam Hussein from power.

Exercise context

Operation: Impact is described by the Government of Canada as the CAF's role in the international coalition to assist local security forces who are fighting against Daesh in the Republic of Iraq and Syria. The operation has four main contributions: CAF members operate an all-source intelligence centre for Joint Task Force-Iraq; CAF members from the Canadian Special Operations Forces Command train, advise and assist Iraqi security forces; and CAF has sent training assistance teams to Jordan and Lebanon to help stabilize and secure the region through capacity building of their armed forces.

The Global Coalition was formed in September 2014 with 77 other committed states. It is committed to tackling Daesh, which is a terrorist organization also known by the acronyms ISIS, IS, and ISIL. The coalition was created to respond to Daesh making significant progress in taking control of territory in Iraq and Syria, including the capture of Fallujah, in early 2014.

Figure 7

How much territory IS has lost since January 2015

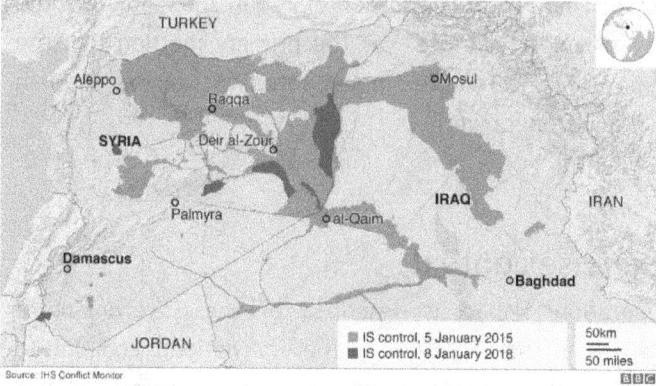

(Map Source: https://www.bbc.com/news/world-middle-east-27838034)

Competence examination

Candidates should be able to use a QIC to accurately conduct intelligence analysis and therefore prepare them to create reliable intelligence products for decision makers. Candidates will have a complete understanding of when, why, and how to use a quality of information check, as well as an ability to apply this knowledge correctly in a working environment using the matrix.

All Media Pack information for analysis can be found in the Media Pack section under Chapter 3.

Chapter 4. Indicators and Signposts of Change

Natalie Archutowski,
Marco Autelitano, &
Emma Curtis

Tasks

001 - Training objectives

002 - What is an ISP

003 - When to use an ISP

004 - How to use an ISP

005 - Benefits of an ISP

006 - Limitations of an ISP

007 - Example of an ISP matrix

008 - Table top exercise scenario

009 - Exercise context

010 - Competence examination

011 - Candidates analyze provided sources and conduct an ISP

012 - Candidates present to panel for competency evaluation using GRINTSUM

Training objective

The training objective is to familiarize candidates with the use of SAT, specifically, the use of an ISP, in order for members to accurately conduct intelligence analysis and therefore prepare them to create reliable intelligence products for decision makers.

What is an ISP

An ISP is a type of diagnostic analytic technique used to reduce cognitive bias and aid in forecasting the likelihood of increased risk or potential threats in a given scenario. ISP's can help reduce the chances of analysts overlooking seemingly small events that may prove to have relevance later on in a mission. Once indicators are identified, monitoring a situation overtime allows analysts to better predict the direction in which a security situation is heading.

When to use an ISP

The ISP matrix can be useful for determining how likely security threats are to arise in a given region, or if an existing threat is likely to decrease or increase. It can also be helpful with outlining the conditions and expected events or incidents that could signify a higher probability of particular outcomes occurring. Once the criteria for indicators is created, monitoring it over time is relatively straightforward. Analysts continue to monitor and add to the matrix to help reduce surprise, since a variety of potential hypotheses have been considered at the outset.

How to use an ISP

1. Determine your security question/hypothesis
2. Identify indicators
3. Create your matrix – use indicators in rows and years in columns
4. Determine the relevance key that will be used to evaluate Indicators
5. Evaluate sources using the predetermined key
6. Ensure sources are reliable or corroborated
7. Draw conclusions from the evaluated indicators

Benefits of an ISP

The ISP Matrix can be used in combination with other SATs such as a key assumption check, quality of information check, a "what if" or a High Impact/Low Probability analysis. Therefore, it can reduce surprise and can increase the foreseeability of low probability/high impact type events, when and if they occur. This would in turn allow for the candidates to be more prepared for unlikely events and for anticipating a changing security situation. Rather than merely reacting as changes occur or being caught by surprise at "sudden" developments.

Limitations of an ISP

ISPs can be time-consuming, particularly in the creation of the Matrix. Since the list of factors to be considered for each hypothesis or potential threat that is under consideration can potentially be quite large. Therefore, this could require more time and resources for the proper application of the technique. The presence of time may not be available in certain circumstances or mission parameters. The possibility that surprise may still occur is also a factor if a potential threat is not considered by intelligence analysts or the correct indicators are not correctly determined. Furthermore, the successful implementation of the technique assumes that a consensus can be formed as to what would constitute an "objective indicator" for a particular threat.

Example of an ISP matrix

TOPICS	INDICATORS	2012 I	2012 II	2012 III	2012 IV	2013 I	2013 II	2013 III	2013 IV	2017 I	2017 II	2017 III	2017 IV	2018 I	2018 II
Non-governmental group conflicts (pan/ethnic)	Tuareg ethnic group actively seeking control over Azawad Region (North)	5	5	5	5	2	2	2	2	2	2	3	2	1	1
	Tuareg group MNLA split from partner Islamist organizations to control Azawad Region	4	5	5	5	5	5	5	5	5	4	3	2	1	1
Operation of terrorist organizations	Attacks on civilians	3	3	4	3	3	3	3	3	3	5	5	5	5	5
	Attacks on UN personnel	4	4	4	3	3	3	3	3	3	3	4	4	4	4
	Presence of organized crime	3	3	4	4	4	4	4	4	4	3	3	4	4	4
	Presence of terrorist groups	2	2	3	3	2	2	2	3	3	3	3	3	3	3
Infrastructure and Economic Conditions	Military coup	5	5	4	5	2	2	3	3	3	5	5	5	5	5
	GDP Per Capita PPP	4	4	4	3	3	3	3	3	3	3	3	3	3	3
	Military Expenditure	5	5	5	4	4	4	4	4	4	4	4	4	4	4
	Prevalance of drug trafficking	5	5	5	5	4	4	4	4	4	4	2	2	2	2
	Access to Government services	1	1	1	1	1	1	1	1	1	1	3	3	2	2
	Recruitment of child soldiers	2	2	2	2	2	2	2	2	2	2	3	2	4	4
	Basic education	5	5	5	4	4	4	4	4	5	5	5	5	5	5
Governmental Capacity	Lack of inclusive mechanisms in the management of public affairs	1	1	2	3	5	5	5	4	4	4	5	5	3	3
	Adherence to the constitution	5	5	5	5	4	4	4	4	4	4	4	3	3	4
	Rule of law	1	1	1	1	3	3	3	3	3	3	2	2	3	3
	Necessity of foreign intervention	2	2	2	2	2	2	2	2	2	3	3	3	3	3

KEY
1 = negligible concern
2 = low concern
3 = moderate concern
4 = substantial concern
5 = serious concern

Table top exercise: ISP

Exercise scenario

Based upon the factors of destabilization in Mali, to what extent does a security risk exist for CAF Operations in Mali, what other factors should be accounted for, and what are the potential implications that should be considered?

Exercise context

As there is an ongoing CAF operation currently ongoing in Mali, the current and long-term security environment in Mali is of particular relevance and is thus the focus of this exercise. In 2012 and 2013, political and ethnic groups staged a coup that resulted in foreign interference from France and the United Nations. The situation in Mali has once again resurfaced as a prime topic in world news, possibly pointing to changes in the security environment. The ISP is suited especially well to this situation as we have empirical evidence of what indicators an unstable Mali exhibited in 2012 and 2013, which we can compare to the current period. By using the ISP technique, the long-term security outlook in Mali can be forecast, and changes to the security environment can be predicted in advance. Particularly by monitoring factors that can be otherwise difficult to detect, which may in turn influence the security environment. Factors such as a decrease in the overall availability of government services for the population, or a change in the nation's GDP per capita are examples of subtle changes, that may be overlooked and that an ISP will track. Therefore, the use of this technique can potentially assist the CAF in planning and conducting operations in Mali. As well as assisting the CAF in protecting the personnel who are deployed to Mali and operating directly in the theater of operation.

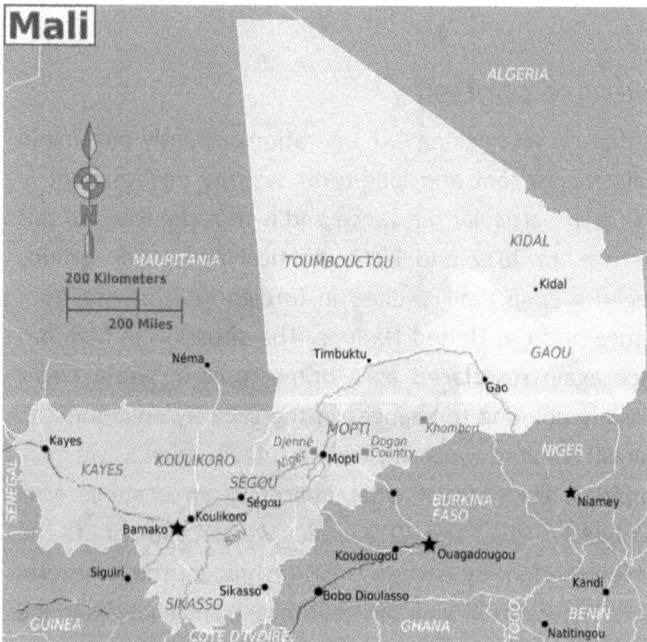

(Source: https://www.mapsland.com/africa/mali/large-regions-map-of-mali)

Competence examination

Candidates will be assessed on their ability to: identify what an indicator is, generate an ISP matrix, generate a Graphical summary using the ISP matrix, deliver an assessment of a security problem, based on the results of the ISP matrix and graphical summary.

All Media Pack information for analysis can be found in the Media Pack section under Chapter 4.

Chapter 5: Analysis of Competing Hypothesis
Caitlin Manz & Asha Khera

Tasks

001 - Training objectives

002 - What is an ACH

003 - When to use an ACH

004 - Why use an ACH

005 - How to use an ACH matrix

006 - Steps

007 - Benefits of an ACH

008 - Limitations of an ACH

009 - Example of an ACH table

010 - Table top exercise scenario

011 - Exercise terminology

012 - Exercise context

013 - Competence examination

014 - Candidates analyze provided sources and conduct an ACH

015 - Candidates present to panel for competency evaluation using GRINTSTUM

Adapted from University of Texas.

Training objectives

The training objective is to enhance candidates' skills in using structured analytic techniques (SATs), specifically focusing on an ACH. This training's goal is for members to accurately conduct intelligence analysis and therefore, prepare them to create reliable intelligence products for decision makers.

What is an ACH

An ACH is a type of diagnostic SAT used to aid analysts' judgement on important issues, which require a careful weighing of alternative explanations/hypotheses. An ACH helps to minimize and potentially overcome cognitive limitations, as well as avoid common analytic pitfalls. It also forces the analyst to identify a variety of alternative explanations at the outset of a project, and evaluate all of the according evidence, seeking to <u>disconfirm</u> rather than confirm hypotheses. There are numerous types of ACH's, such as Bayesian, Automated, and Manual.

When to use an ACH

An ACH is a highly effective technique when there is a large amount of data to absorb and evaluate. While a single analyst can use an ACH, it is most effective with a small team that can challenge each other's evaluation of the evidence and help come up with alternative explanations. An ACH is particularly appropriate for controversial issues when analysts want to develop a clear record that shows what theories they have considered and how they arrived at their judgments. Developing the ACH matrix allows other analysts (or even policy-makers) to review their analysis and identify areas of agreement and disagreement. Evidence can also be examined more systematically, and analysts have found that this makes the technique ideal for considering the possibility of deception and denial, as well as aiding in eliminating confirmation bias.

Why use an ACH

An ACH differs from other SATs in three ways:

An ACH requires that you identify and analyze a variety of alternative hypotheses at the outset of an analytical project, rather than focus on a single conclusion.

The objective of an ACH is to refute or eliminate hypotheses, whereas other SATs generally seek to confirm a favored hypothesis.

An ACH forces the analyst to evaluate each item of evidence, in terms of their diagnostic value and credibility, as well as whether that piece of evidence is <u>consistent, inconsistent or not applicable</u> with each of the hypotheses.

How to use an ACH matrix

Terminology:

Inconsistency Score (IS): Consistent with the principle of refuting hypotheses, only the inconsistent evidence is counted in an ACH. An Inconsistent (I) item of evidence counts as -1 thus, the hypothesis with the highest negative number is disconfirmed in that order. The hypothesis with an IS of closest to 0 is the most likely scenario/explanation. Consistent ratings (C) nor non-applicable ratings (N/A) do not count towards the inconsistency score.

Weighting: The "diagnostic value" of the evidence is determined as analysts evaluate whether a piece of evidence is found to be consistent with only one hypothesis or could support more than one, or indeed all hypotheses. It essentially determines how much weight that piece of evidence should have in the analysis. It is scored by <u>Highly Diagnostic and Less Diagnostic.</u>

Highly Diagnostic: Evidence is consistent with ONE hypothesis

Less Diagnostic: Evidence may lend itself to being consistent with <u>more than one</u> hypothesis or is non-applicable to some hypotheses.

Source Credibility Score: The credibility of sources should be evaluated at all times. The reliability will be scored using a scale of A, B, C, D & F.

A: Completely reliable - No doubt regarding authenticity, trustworthiness, integrity, competence. History of complete reliability.

B: Usually reliable - Some doubt regarding authenticity or trustworthiness or integrity or competence (one count). History of general reliability.

C: Fairly reliable - Doubt regarding authenticity, trustworthiness, integrity, competence (two counts and more). History of occasional reliability.

D: Usually not reliable. Definite doubt regarding authenticity, trustworthiness, integrity, competence. History of occasional reliability.

F: Not reliable - Certainty about lack of authenticity, trustworthiness, integrity, competence. History of unreliability.

Steps

1. Divide reading materials amongst team members and scan briefly to familiarize team on recent happenings/events.

2. Brainstorm amongst team to identify 3 possible hypotheses (*including 1 null).

3. Create arguments supporting each hypothesis and gather supporting evidence.

4. Prepare a matrix with hypotheses laid horizontally, across the top and each piece of evidence written vertically, along the left side.

5. Determine whether each piece of evidence is consistent (C); inconsistent (I); or neutral (not applicable) (N). This process allows for seeing that some evidence will be consistent with more than one hypothesis and be less valuable in disproving hypotheses.

6. Refine the matrix and reconsider the hypotheses—determine if new hypotheses are needing to be added and re-examine the information available.

7. Talley the pieces of evidence that are inconsistent and consistent with each hypothesis to see which explanations are the weakest and strongest.

8. Analyze how sensitive the ACH results are to a few critical items of evidence; should those pieces prove to be wrong, misleading, or subject to deception, how would it impact an explanation's validity?

9. Ask what evidence is not being seen but would be expected for a given hypothesis to be true. Evaluate if denial and deception is a possibility.
10. Establish the likelihood for the hypotheses and report all the conclusions, including the weaker hypotheses that should still be monitored as new information becomes available.
11. Explore & report for what could account for inconsistent data.

Benefits of an ACH

ACH helps analysts overcome three common mistakes that can lead to inaccurate forecasts:

Analysts often are susceptible to being influenced by a first impression, based on incomplete data, an existing analytic line, or a single explanation that seems to fit well enough.

Analysts seldom generate a full set of explanations or hypotheses at the outset of a project.

Analysts often rely on evidence to support their preferred hypothesis, but which also is consistent with other explanations.

Limitations of an ACH

One of the limitations of an ACH is that it does not provide a basis for taking assumptions into account. Another limitation is that it is easy to be biased in choice of examples/evidence, as well as in weighting of evidence. Finally, an ACH is neither prescriptive, nor policy-guiding. In this sense, it does not necessarily tell a policymaker what to do, rather it aids in the potential explanation of what is least likely to have occurred, regarding a security problem.

Example of an ACH table

Security Question: *Is Lone Wolf Terrorism on the rise?*

Hypothesis 1: YES, Lone wolf terrorism is on the rise.

Hypothesis 2: NO, lone wolf terrorism is disappearing.

Hypothesis 3: NULL, the rate of lone wolf terrorism is stagnant.

	EVIDENCE	CREDIBILITY	WEIGHT	H1	H2	H3
IS:				-3.0	-1.0	-4.0
E1	The Charlottesville Virginia Vehicle Attack - USA (2017)	A	Highly Diagnostic	I	C	I
E2	The Manchester Arena Bombing - UK (2017)	B	Less Diagnostic	N/A	C	I
E3	The Finsbury Park Drive-by Mosque Attack UK (2018)	B	Highly Diagnostic	I	C	I
E4	The Quebec City Mosque Shooting - Canada (2017)	B	Highly Diagnostic	I	C	I

Table top exercise: ACH

Exercise scenario

This chapter's security question is - *Does the increasing presence of the Night Wolves Motorcycle Club (NWMC) in post-Soviet states influence the likelihood of kinetic activity amongst host populations?*

Exercise terminology

Night Wolves Motorcycle Club (NWMC): The NWMC is declared to be the first independent motorcycle club in Russia.

Kinetic Activity: the use or preparation for use of force against another state or group. This process is the more classical method of engaging in kinetic warfare

Exercise context

The NWMC declared to be the first independent motorcycle club in Russia in 1989 (Zabyelina, 2017). Founded and lead by Alexander Zaldostanov, the NWMC embraces Orthodox Christian beliefs, and propagates ultranationalist ideals (Zabyelina, 2017). Zaldostanov asserts that their goal is to fight against American democracy, and unite Russian compatriots and lands in post-Soviet states (Zabyelina,

2017). He refers to the annexation of Crimea as one of the first steps towards realizing this mission (Zabyelina, 2017).

The NWMC contains approximately 5,000 members domestically, with chapters in nearly all major Russian cities (Harris, 2018; Zabyelina, 2017). The club claims to have over sixty-five chapters in over ten countries, including Belarus, Bulgaria, Germany, Macedonia, Romania, Serbia, and the Ukraine (Harris, 2018; Lauder, 2018; Zabyelina, 2017).

The NWMC contains corporate entities, as well as subsequent umbrella companies and Non-Governmental Organizations (NGOs) (Harris, 2018; Zabyelina, 2017). These are utilized to provide opportunities for legitimate social engagement with the public, law enforcement and political parties, in an effort for the NWMC to appear legitimized as a genuine business or political entity (Harris, 2018). These organizations also function as a 'covert' connection between the club and the Kremlin, as they have received numerous multi-million-ruble government grants for different social projects (Harris, 2018).

These organizations also function as forms of soft and hard power for Russia. The NWMC's youth NGO Night Wolves MANO, works as a soft propaganda campaign aimed at a young demographic, promoting anti-Western views and pro-Russian nationalism domestically, as well as in Crimea (Harris, 2018; Zabyelina, 2017). The NWMC, furthermore, contains security companies offering tactical military training, martial arts training, and other security services in Russia, and abroad (Harris, 2018).

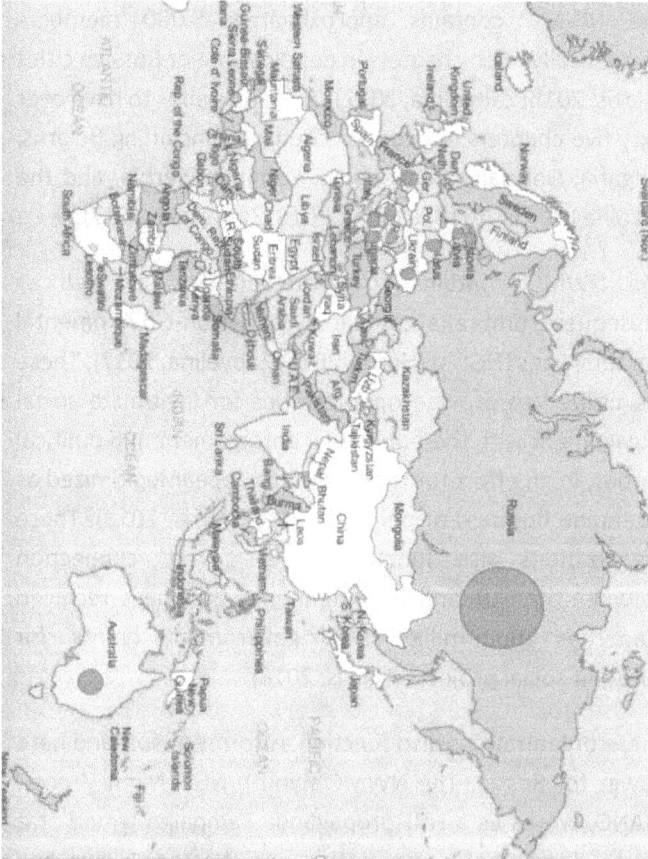

(Dots indicate areas of heightened NWMC activity – map source: shutterstock.com/worldmap (2018))

Competence examination

Candidates should be able to use an ACH to identify alternative explanations (hypotheses) and evaluate any/all evidence that disconfirms rather than confirms hypotheses. Candidates will be able to use an ACH to help minimize and potentially overcome cognitive limitations, as well as avoid common analytic pitfalls. Further, Candidates will be able to make an ACH matrix and represent that in a GRINTSUM

All Media Pack information for analysis can be found in the Media Pack section under Chapter 5.

Chapter 6. Cross Impact Matrix

Evan Pearce &
Rob van den Boom

Tasks

001 - Training objective

002 - What is a CIM

003 - When to use a CIM

004 - Why use a CIM

005 - How to use a CIM

006 - Steps

007 - Benefits of a CIM

008 - Limitations of a CIM

009 - Example of CIM

010 - Table top exercise scenario

011 - Exercise context

012 - Competence examination

013 - Candidates analyze provided sources and conduct a CIM

014 - Candidates present to panel for competency evaluation using GRINTSUM.

Training objective

Candidates should be able to confidently employ the Cross-Impact Matrix (CIM) Structured Analytical Technique to add value to future research questions they may face.

What is a CIM

The Cross-Impact Matrix is an analytical technique which assesses how variables impact one another, thus providing a model to reduce future uncertainty.

When to use a CIM

The Cross-Impact Matrix is ideal in complex scenarios where many interrelated variables are present.

Regardless if the scenario is constantly changing, stable, or following a significant event, this technique remains useful in analyzing how variables interact.

The CIM should be used early in the investigative process, following the preliminary brainstorming of variables.

Why use a CIM

A Cross-Impact Matrix forces analysts to break down a scenario into its variable parts. The matrix then places each variable in a table to visualize how it is impacted by other variables.

How to use a CIM

Terminology

Weighting: The "diagnostic value" of the evidence is determined as analysts evaluate whether a piece of evidence is found to have a strong positive impact (5), positive impact (4), neutral impact (3), negative impact (2), strong negative impact (1).

Steps

1. Divide reading materials amongst team members and familiarize them on the scenario.
2. Brainstorm amongst team to identify 6-7 variables to include in your matrix.
3. Prepare a matrix, the same variables should descend top to bottom on the left side of the table and extend in identical order from left to right along to top.

4. Begin with your first variable, it should be the leftmost variable in the top row. We are assessing the impact of the individual variables from the top row on the individual variables in the left-most column.
5. Determine whether the effect is strong positive, positive, neutral, negative or strong negative. (Specifically, is there a strong positive effect, a positive effect, no effect, a negative effect or a strong negative effect).
6. Examine the matrix for variables which have strong impact.
7. Assess why/how variables are likely to cause changes in the future, ask if the matrix supports or challenges your hypothesis?

Benefits of a CIM

A CIM establishes a uniform understanding of the variables in play. The use of a team mitigates the effect bias can have on the assessment. Evaluating a scenario based on its variables ensures that results are as accurate as they can be. After assessing the interconnectedness between variables, you can reasonably predict how a given event is likely to impact your scenario.

Limitations of a CIM

The process of selecting variables and weighing their impact is subjective and therefore inserts bias into the analysts' assessment of the scenario.

Analysts must be knowledgeable about the scenario, since the absence of an important variable in the matrix can severely weaken an intelligence product.

Example of a CIM table

Impact of → on ↓ Scale: 1 to 5	Right wing groups are attacking and will be prepared	Attack carried out easily	Attacks will be larger in scale	Vandalism of opposition property	Increase in number of attacks
Right wing groups are attacking and will be prepared	-	5	4	1	2
Attack carried out easily	4	-	2	1	5
Attacks will be larger in scale	1	2	-	1	3
Vandalism of opposition property	3	2	1	-	1
Increase in number of attacks	2	4	1	1	-
Passive Sum					

Table top exercise: CIM
Exercise scenario

This chapter's security question is - *What is the nature of the security threat faced by Canadian Armed Forces stationed in Latvia from Russian hybrid warfare tactics?*

Exercise context

The Canadian Armed Forces (CAF) deployed its first Hornet Air Task Force group to Eastern Europe in 2014 as part of its NATO contribution in the region. In 2017, the CAF took the lead on an enhanced forward battle group in Latvia as part of its Operation: Reassurance. The operation was established to reassure Canada's NATO allies and to deter the perceived threat from Russian aggression and expansionism. Essentially, the purpose of the mission is to establish a buffer zone between Latvia and Russia. 7 other nations are also present. Currently, there are 455 CAF members deployed and that number is scheduled to increase to 540. The mission is slated to continue until March 2023.

In an era of perceived Russian aggression against the West, academics, policymakers, intelligence analysts, and soldiers must assess and act on intelligence regarding the preservation of Canadian and NATO values in the region.

Therefore, we have structured a Cross-impact Matrix that can assess the situation and hypothesize possible futures by examining individual variables. This allows us to make the best decision possible by using a predictive structured analytic technique.

Consider in Hypotheses

Which tactics are used in hybrid warfare? How does a hybrid warfare strategy further Russian policy aims? How do these variables affect one another?

Mission timeline:

April 29, 2014 – the CAF sent its first CF-188 Hornet Air Task Force to Europe. Since then, the CAF had periodically sent air task forces to Central and Eastern Europe.

May 3, 2014 – the CAF sent a Land Task Force to Central and Eastern Europe, based in Poland.

May 13, 2014 – the CAF sent a Maritime Task Force of one frigate to Central and Eastern Europe.

June 19, 2017 – Canadian-led NATO enhanced Forward Presence battlegroup Latvia was stood up during a ceremony at Camp Adazi, Latvia.

August 17, 2017 – The Land Task Force in Poland completed its final deployment.

July 10, 2018 – The Prime Minister of Canada announced the renewal of Canada's contribution to NATO's enhanced Forward Presence until March 2023. The CAF will also increase the number of members deployed to Latvia from 455 to 540.

Competence examination

Candidates should be able to create a CIM. Further, identify and present conclusions they have derived from their analysis of variables by using a Cross-Impact Matrix. Finally, candidates should be able to represent those findings in the form of a GRINTSUM.

All Media Pack information for analysis can be found in the Media Pack section under Chapter 6.

Blank templates

Chapter 2 – Key Assumptions Check

Assumptions	Assessment

Chapter 3 – Quality of Information Check

	A	B	C	D
5				
4				
3				
2				
1				
0				

Chapter 4 – Indicators and Signposts of Change

TOPICS	INDICATORS	(INSERT YEAR)	(INSERT YEAR)	(INSERT TREND YEAR)	(INSERT TREND YEAR)	KEY:
		I II III IV	I II III IV	III IV	I II	1 = Negligible concern 2 = Low Concern 3 = Moderate Concern 4 = Substantial Concern 5 = serious Concern

Chapter 5 – Analysis of Competing Hypothesis

	Inconsistency Score:	E1	E2	E3	E4	E5	ETC.
EVIDENCE							
CREDIBILITY (of source)							
WEIGHT							
H1							
H2							
H3							

Hypothesis 1:

Hypothesis 2:

Hypothesis 3:

Chapter 6 – Cross Impact Matrix

	Evidence 1	Evidence 2	Evidence 3	Evidence 4
Evidence 1				
Evidence 2				
Evidence 3				
Evidence 4				
Evidence 5 & so on				

CIM Legend

+	Strong Positive
+	Positive
	Neutral
-	Negative
■	Strong Negative

References

Aydin, B., & Ozleblebici, Z. (2015). Should we rely on intelligence cycle? *Journal of Military and Information Science, 3(3),* 93-99. doi:10.17858/jmisci.78166

Chang, W., Berdini, E., Mandel, D.R., & Tetlock, P.E. (2018). Restructuring structured analytic techniques in intelligence. *Intelligence and National Security*, 33:3, 337-356. doi: 10.1080/02684527.2017.1400230

Coulthart, S. (2016). Why do analysts use structured analytic techniques? An in-depth study of an American intelligence agency. *Intelligence and National Security*, 31:7, 933-9948. doi: 10.1080/02684527.2016.1140327

George, R., Bruce, J. (2014). *Analyzing Intelligence: National Security Practitioners' Perspectives.* Second Edition. Washington, D.C., Georgetown University Press.

Heuer, R., Pherson, R. (2010). Structured Analytic Techniques for Intelligence Analysis. *CQ Press.*

Kelshall, C. *Week 4: The analyst and analytical tradecraft* [PowerPoint slides]. Retrieved from https://canvas.sfu.ca/courses/39511/files/folder/LECTURES?preview=8017298

Networking European Citizenship Education. (2016). *Key Assumptions Check*. Retrieved from https://www.bpb.de/system/files/dokument_pdf/ Scenario%20Presentation%20by%20Oliver%20Gna d.pdf

United Nations. (2011). Criminal intelligence: Manual for analysts. *United Nation Office on Drugs and Crime.* Retrieved from https://canvas.sfu.ca/courses/39511/files/folder/ week%204%20readings?preview=801724 1

US Government. (2009, March). *A tradecraft primer: Structured analytic techniques for improving intelligence analysis*. Retrieved from https://www.cia.gov/library/center-for-the-study- of-intelligence/csi-publications/books- and- monographs/Tradecraft%20Primer-apr09.pdf

Walton, T. (2010). *Challenges in Intelligence Analysis: Lessons from 1300 BCE to the Present*. Cambridge, United Kingdom. Cambridge University Press.

Chapter 2. Media Pack

Chang, W., Berdini, E., Mandel, D.R., & Tetlock, P.E. (2018). Restructuring structured analytic techniques in intelligence. Intelligence and National Security, 33:3, 337-356. doi: 10.1080/02684527.2017.1400230

Coulthart, S. (2016). Why do analysts use structured analytic techniques? An in-depth study of an American intelligence agency. *Intelligence and National Security, 31:7*, 933-9948. doi:10.1080/02684527.2016.1140327

Jason Wilson (2018, January,18). Burst your bubble: Australia's 'African gang crisis' has been brewing for years. Retrieved from https://www.theguardian.com/australia-news/commentisfree/2018/jan/18/the-african-gang-crisis-has-been-brewing-in-australias-media-for-years

Jason Wilson (2016, October,28). Fear and loathing on the streets: the Soldiers of Odin and the rise of anti-refugee vigilantes. Retrieved from https://www.theguardian.com/commentisfree/2016/oct/28/fear-and-loathing-on-the-streets-the-soldiers-of-odin-and-the-rise-of-anti-refugee-vigilantes

Kauranen, A., Cortellessa, E., Ahren, R., Wootliff, R., Gross, & J. A., Mounes. (2016, February, 10). Finland's neo-Nazis face off against pro-refugee huggers.

Retrieved from
https://www.timesofisrael.com/finlands-neo-nazis-face-off-against-pro-refugee-huggers/

Lamoureux, M. (2016, September 06). Soldiers of Odin, European 'extreme anti-refugee group,' sets up chapters in Canada | CBC News. Retrieved from https://www.cbc.ca/news/canada/edmonton/soldiers-of-odin-dubbed-extreme-anti-refugee-group-patrol-edmonton-streets-1.3745493

Mack Lamoureux (2016, April,15). Soldiers of Odin, Europe's Notorious Anti-Immigration Group, Beginning to Form Cells in Canada. Retrieved from https://www.vice.com/en_ca/article/gqma9m/soldiers-of-odin-europes-notorious-anti-immigration-group-beginning-to-form-cells-in-canada

Perry, B., Scrivens, R. (2017). Resisting the right: Countering right-wing extremism in Canada. Canadian Journal of Criminology and Criminal Justice, 59(4), 534-558. doi:10.3138/cjccj.2016.0029

Public Safety Canada. (2017). Public report on the Terrorist threat to Canada. https://www.publicsafety.gc.ca/cnt/rsrcs/pblctns/pblc-rprt-trrrst-thrt-cnd-2017/index-en.aspx

R. (2017, April 02). Soldiers of Odin vs anti-racists: Protesters clash in Toronto. Retrieved from: https://www.youtube.com/watch?v=j_nSBjFpVKs

CASIS Vancouver

Reuters & Vice News (2016, March,02). The Anti-
Immigrant 'Soldiers of Odin' Are Expanding Across
Europe. Retrieved from
https://news.vice.com/article/the-anti-immigrant-
soldiers-of-odin-are-expanding-across-europe

Russia Today (2016, February,26). Trouble in Valhalla?
New 'Soldiers of Allah' set to counter 'infidel'
'Soldiers of Odin' in Norway. Retrieved from
https://www.rt.com/news/333767-norway-
vigilante-soldiers-allah/

Russia Today (2016, April,03). Estonian politician wants
Koran banned in public places. Retrieved from
https://www.rt.com/news/338252-estonia-
politician-ban-koran/

Russia Today (2016, March,27). Vehicles set ablaze for 2nd
night amid riots in Stockholm suburb. Retrieved
from https://www.rt.com/news/337334-
stockholm-migrant-suburb-riots-fire/

Sputnik News (2018, August,09). Finnish Police Fence-
Sitting as Anti-Crime Soldiers of Odin Patrol Aland
Isles. Retrieved from
https://sputniknews.com/europe/2018080910670
65046-finland-aland-soldiers-odin-patrols/

Sputnik News (2016, January,15). Finnish Anti-Immigration
Militia Counterproductive, Impede Police Work.
Retrieved from

https://sputniknews.com/europe/2016011510331
96356-finland-militia-police/

Sputnik News (2016, January,15). Refugee Fears Bring Anti-
Immigrant 'Soldiers of Odin' to Finnish Streets.
Retrieved from
https://sputniknews.com/europe/2016011510331
90010-finland-refugee-crisis-patrols/

Sputnik News (2016, Feburary,25). Rising Unrest: Anti-
Immigrant 'Soldiers of Odin" Take Over Estonian
Capital. Retrieved from
https://sputniknews.com/europe/2016022510353
31614-anti-immigration-march-tallinn/

Sputnik News (2016, March,22). Viking Vigilantes: Crime-
Fighting Soldiers of Odin Expand to Sweden.
Retrieved from
https://sputniknews.com/europe/2016032210367
41831-sweden-finland-soldiers-of-odin/

Chapter 3. Media Pack

Adel, L. (2016, January 18). Sajjan: Canada to withdraw from international coalition's operations. *Iraqi News.* Retrieved from https://www.iraqinews.com/baghdad-politics/canada-to-withdraw-from-coalitions-operations/

Aljazeera. (2018, August 22). ISIL leader urges followers to keep fighting in new recording. Retrieved from https://www.aljazeera.com/news/2018/08/isil-leader-urges-followers-fighting-recording-180822202049824.html

Aljazeera. (2018, August 29). Iraq: Eight killed in Anbar province suicide bombing. Retrieved from https://www.aljazeera.com/news/2018/08/iraq-killed-anbar-province-suicide-bombing-180829072538649.html

Aydin, B., & Ozleblebici, Z. (2015). Should we rely on intelligence cycle? *Journal of Military and Information Science, 3(3),* 93-99. doi:10.17858/jmisci.78166

Bell, S., & Russell, A. (2018, July 3). Government should be more open about targeting of Canadian ISIS fighters, former JAG says. *Global News.* Retrieved from https://globalnews.ca/news/4308746/more-open-about-targeting-jag-says/

Brown, S. (2010). Likert scale examples for surveys. *Iowa State University Extension.* Retrieved from

https://www.extension.iastate.edu/Documents/A
NR/LikertScaleExamplesforSurveys.pdf

Canadian Press. (2016, February 19). Communications
security establishment, Canada's electronic spy
service, takes prominent role against ISIS.
Huffington Post. Retrieved from
https://www.huffingtonpost.ca/2016/02/19/cana
da-s-electronic-spies-at-the-centre-of-beefed-up-
isil-intelligence-
effort_n_9267002.html?utm_hp_ref=ca-
operation-impact

Canadian Press. (2017, July 4). Canada's special forces
working on 'borrowed time': Deputy commander.
Huffington Post. Retrieved from
https://www.huffingtonpost.ca/2017/07/04/cana
das-special-forces-working-on-borrowed-time-
deputy-comma_a_23015853/?utm_hp_ref=ca-
operation-impact.

Canadian Forces Videos. "Operation IMPACT." YouTube,
YouTube, 17 Jan. 2017,
www.youtube.com/watch?v=ZVakmnmDhDI.

Ebraheem, M. (2018, March 6). NATO troops staying in
Iraq at Baghdad's request, says chief. *Iraqi News.*
Retrieved from https://www.iraqinews.com/iraq-
war/nato-troops-staying-in-iraq-at-baghdads-
request-says-chief/

Ferran, L. (2016, April 7). One third of Iraqis think US
supports terrorism, ISIS. *ABC News.* Retrieved
from
https://abcnews.go.com/International/iraqis-us-
supports-terrorism-isis/story?id=38220207

Government of Canada. (2017, January 26). *Statements
from the technical briefing on January 26, 2017 to
provide an update on Canada's engagement in
Iraq and the region.* Retrieved from
http://www.forces.gc.ca/en/news/article.page?do
c=statements-from-the-technical-briefing-on-
january-26-2017-to-provide-an-update-on-
canada-s-engagement-in-iraq-and-the-
region/ix1xz1u4

Government of Canada. (2018, June 11). *Operation Impact.*
Retrieved from
http://www.forces.gc.ca/en/operations-abroad-
current/op-impact.page

Kelshall, C. *Week 4: The analyst and analytical tradecraft*
[PowerPoint slides]. Retrieved from
https://canvas.sfu.ca/courses/39511/files/folder/
LECTURES?preview=8017298

Mostafa, M. (2017, June 29). Canada extends Iraq mission
by 2 years, 200 troops involved. *Iraqi News.*
Retrieved from https://www.iraqinews.com/iraq-
war/canada-extends-iraq-mission-2-years-200-
troops-involved/

Mostafa, N. (2018, June 9). Peshmerga says informed about Canada suspending troops training from media. *Iraqi News*. Retrieved from https://www.iraqinews.com/iraq-war/peshmerga-says-informed-about-canada-suspending-troops-training-from-media/

Pepeperezcanyear. (2018, July). ISIS hunter: "We are not-superheroes, we are tired of war and we just want to live a decent life" [Post 281]. Message posted tohttps://www.reddit.com/r/syriancivilwar/comments/8rjt1r/isis_hunter_we_are_not_superheroes_we_are_tired/

Pugliese, D. (2015, July 6). Some military personnel question hardship and risk allowances on operation impact. *Ottawa Citizen*. Retrieved from https://ottawacitizen.com/news/national/defence-watch/some-military-personnel-question-hardship-and-risk-allowances-on-operation-impact

Sputnik. (2018, March 20). 'The US has done nothing but create misery for Iraqi people' - academic. Retrieved from https://sputniknews.com/analysis/201803201062738468-us-create-misery-iraqi-people/

Williams, J. (2018, September 8). The violent protests in Iraq, explained. Vox. Retrieved from https://www.vox.com/world/2018/9/7/17831526

/iraq-protests-basra-burning-government-
buildings-iran-consulate-water

United Nations Security Council. (2018). *Twenty-second
report of the Analytical Support and Sanctions
Monitoring Team submitted pursuant to
resolution 2368 (2017) concerning ISIL (Da'esh),
Al-Qaida and associated individuals and entities.*
Retrieved from http://undocs.org/S/2018/705.

United Nations. (2011). Criminal intelligence: Manual for
analysts. *United Nation Office on Drugs and Crime.*
Retrieved from
https://canvas.sfu.ca/courses/39511/files/folder/
week%204%20readings?preview=8017241

US Government. (2009, March). *A tradecraft primer:
Structured analytic techniques for improving
intelligence analysis.* Retrieved from
https://www.cia.gov/library/center-for-the-study-
of-intelligence/csi-publications/books-and-
monographs/Tradecraft%20Primer-apr09.pdf

Chapter 4. Media Pack

Abderrahmane, Abdelkader. (2012). Drug Trafficking and
	the Crisis in Mali. Retrieved from
	https://www.globalpolicy.org/component/conten
	t/article/190-issues/51838-drug-trafficking-and-
	the-crisis-in-mali.html

Al Jazeera. (2013). Mali Frees Tuareg Rebel-Linked
	Prisoners. Retrieved from
	https://www.aljazeera.com/news/africa/2013/10/
	mali-tuareg-prisoners-
	2013102232924835201.html

Al Jazeera. (2018). Suspected Rebel Fighters Kill Dozens of
	Tuareg in Mali. Retrieved from
	https://www.aljazeera.com/news/2018/04/suspe
	cted-rebel-fighters-kill-dozens-tuareg-mali-
	180429075636520.html

Al Jazeera. (2018, August 20). Constitutional court ratifies
	President Keita's election win. Retrieved from
	https://www.aljazeera.com/news/2018/08/consti
	tutional-court-ratifies-president-keita-election-
	win-180820114526318.html

Al Jazeera. (2018, August 05). Mali: Candidate Soumaila
	Cisse goes to court alleging vote fraud. Retrieved
	from
	https://www.aljazeera.com/news/2018/08/mali-
	candidate-soumaila-cisse-court-alleging-vote-
	fraud-180805154952537.html

BBC. (2013, June 18). Mali and Tuareg rebels sign peace
      deal. Retrieved from
      https://www.bbc.com/news/world-africa-
      22961519

BBC. (2015, June 20). Mali's Tuareg rebels sign peace deal.
      Retrieved from
      https://www.bbc.com/news/world-africa-
      33213931

BBC. (2018, April 28). Mali Tuaregs killed in 'jihadist
      revenge' attacks. Retrieved from
      https://www.bbc.com/news/world-africa-
      43938531

Burke, J. (2018, August 16). Mali's president wins second
      term in country plagued by violence. Retrieved
      from
      https://www.theguardian.com/world/2018/aug/1
      6/malis-president-wins-second-term-in-country-
      plagued-by-violence

Council on Foreign Relations. (2018). Destabilization in
      Mali. Retrieved from
      https://www.cfr.org/interactives/global-conflict-
      tracker#!/conflict/destabilization-of-mali

Chivvis, C. S. (2017, January 12). Mali's Persistent Jihadist
      Problem. Retrieved from
      https://www.rand.org/blog/2017/01/malis-
      persistent-jihadist-problem.html

Diallo, M. (2018). Suspected Jihadists Kill 40 Tuaregs in North Mali - Governor. U.S. News. Retrieved from https://www.usnews.com/news/world/articles/2018-04-28/suspected-jihadists-kill-40-tuaregs-in-north-mali-governor

EIN News. (2018, August 31). Canadian troops deploy to Mali to prop up pro-Western puppet government. Retrieved from https://world.einnews.com/article__detail/country/mali/460538147-canadian-troops-deploy-to-mali-to-prop-up-pro-western-puppetgovernment?vcode=1gih

Freedom House. (2013). Freedom of the Press 2013: Mali. Retrieved from https://freedomhouse.org/report/freedom-press/2013/mali

Freedom House. (2018). Freedom in the World 2018: Mali. Retrieved from https://freedomhouse.org/report/freedom-world/2018/mali

Hasseye, A. (2018). Negotiations with Jihadists? A Radical Idea Gains Currency in Mali. IRIN. Retrieved from https://www.irinnews.org/analysis/2018/04/19/negotiations-jihadists-radical-idea-gains-currency-mali

Hirsch, A. (2013). Mali Signs Controversial Ceasefire Deal With Tuareg Separatist Insurgents. The Guardian.

Retrieved from
https://www.theguardian.com/world/2013/jun/1
9/mali-peace-deal-tuareg-insurgents-aid

Hirsch, A. & Willsher, K. (2013, January 14). Mali conflict:
France has opened gates of hell, say rebels.
Retrieved from
https://www.theguardian.com/world/2013/jan/1
4/mali-conflict-france-gates-hell

Human Rights Watch. (2017). Mali: Events of 2017.
Retrieved from https://www.hrw.org/world-
report/2018/country-chapters/mali

Institute for Economics and Peace. (2018). Global Peace
Index 2018. Retrieved from
http://visionofhumanity.org/app/uploads/2018/0
6/Global-Peace-Index-2018-2.pdf

IRIN. (2018, September 01). Mali Peace Wreckers, Messy
Food Aid, and Well-Meaning Celebrities - the
Cheat Sheet. Retrieved from
https://allafrica.com/stories/201809010098.html

Kelly, F. (2018, July 03). Mali: French forces targeted in
Gao attack. Retrieved from
https://thedefensepost.com/2018/07/01/mali-
france-gao-attack-operation-barkhane/

National Defence. (2014, November 25). Support to French
operations in Mali. Retrieved from

http://www.forces.gc.ca/en/operations-abroad/support-mali.page

Nossiter, A. (2013). Rebels in North Mali Sign Peace Deal Allowing In Government Troops. The New York Times. Retrieved from https://www.nytimes.com/2013/06/19/world/africa/mali-and-rebels-reach-peace-deal.html

Nyirabikali, Gaudence. (2015). Mali Peace Accord: Actors, Issues, and Their Representation. The Stockholm International Peace Institute. Retrieved from https://www.sipri.org/node/385

Molenaar, F. & van Damme, T. (2017, February). Irregular migration and human smuggling networks in Mali. Retrieved from https://www.clingendael.org/sites/default/files/pdfs/irregular_migration_and_human_smuggling_networks_in_mali.pdf

Raineri, L. & Galletti, C. (2016, September). Organised Crime in Mali: Why it Matters for a Peaceful Transition from Conflict. Retrieved from https://www.international-alert.org/sites/default/files/Mali_OrganisedCrime_EN_2016.pdf

Reuters, T. (2018, July 01). Mali car bombing kills 4 civilians, wounds 31 others, including soldiers | CBC News. Retrieved from https://www.cbc.ca/news/world/mali-french-soldiers-car-bomb-attack-1.4730322

Service Canada, S. (2018, August 24). Operation PRESENCE - Mali. Retrieved from https://www.canada.ca/en/services/defence/caf/operations/military-operations/current-operations/op-presence.html

Smith, Duval Alex. (2015). Inside Mali's Human-Trafficking Underworld in Gao. BBC World News. Retrieved from https://www.bbc.com/news/world-africa-32359142

TASS. (2017, October 4). FSB chief praises global partners' cooperation that helped Russia foil terror plots. Retrieved from http://tass.com/politics/968836

TASS. (2018, January 23). Highest number of UN peacekeepers over past 24 years killed in 2017. Retrieved from http://tass.com/world/986385

TASS. (2015, December 11). Lavrov: Islamic State's plans not confined to Middle East. Retrieved from http://tass.com/politics/843451

TASS. (2015, November 21). Mali terror attack rooted in "export of democracy" to Africa - Russia's foreign ministry. Retrieved from http://tass.com/politics/838306

TASS. (2017, October 9). PM Medvedev calls on world community to put aside ambitions and unite to

stamp out IS. Retrieved from
http://tass.com/politics/969593

TASS. (2017, October 31). Russia begins to assist Sahel
region states in fighting terrorism. Retrieved from
http://tass.com/politics/973296

The World Bank. (2017). Education Statistics (EduStats).
Retrieved from
http://datatopics.worldbank.org/education/count
ry/mali

Tobie, A. (2017, July). A fresh perspective on security
concerns among Malian civil society. Retrieved
from
https://www.sipri.org/publications/2017/sipri-
insights-peace-and-security/fresh-perspective-
security-concerns-among-malian-civil-society

Trading Economics. (2018). Mali GDP Per Capita PPP: 1990-
2018. Retrieved from
https://tradingeconomics.com/mali/gdp-per-
capita-ppp

Trading Economics. (2018). Mali Military Expenditure:
1965-2018. Retrieved from
https://tradingeconomics.com/mali/military-
expenditure

United Nations Educational, Scientific, and Cultural
Organization. Report: Mali. Retrieved from
http://uis.unesco.org/country/ml

United Nations Peacekeeping. (2018). MINUSMA Fact Sheet. Retrieved from https://peacekeeping.un.org/en/fatalities.

United Nations Peacekeeping. (2018). Fatalities Fact Sheet. Retrieved from https://peacekeeping.un.org/en/fatalities

U.S. Department of State. (2017). Mali: Office to Monitor and Combat the Trafficking of Persons. Retrieved from https://www.state.gov/j/tip/rls/tiprpt/countries/2017/271237.htm

U.S. Department of State. (2017). 2017 Trafficking in Persons Report. Retrieved from https://www.state.gov/j/tip/rls/tiprpt/2017/index.htm

Whitehouse, B. (2012). The Force of Action: Legitimizing the Coup in Bamako, Mali. Africa Spectrum, 47(2-3), 93-110.

Zounmenou, D. (2013). The National Movement for the Liberation of Azawad factor in the Mali crisis. *African Security Review, 22*(3), 167-174.

Chapter 5. Media Pack

CTK. (2018, July 26). *HN: Pro-Kremlin Night Wolves assist at Slovak paramilitary base*. Retrieved from Pruage Daily Monitor: http://praguemonitor.com/2018/07/26/hn-pro-kremlin-night-wolves-assist-slovak-paramilitary-base

Galeotti, M. (2017). Crimintern: How the Kremlin Uses Russia's Criminal Networks in Europe. Policy Brief No.208. *European Council on Foreign Relations.* Retrieved from https://www.ecfr.eu/page/-/ECFR208_-_CRIMINTERM_HOW_RUSSIAN_ORGANISED_CRIME_OPERATES_IN_EUROPE02.pdf

Harris, K. (2018). Russia's Fifth Column: The influence of Night Wolves Motorcycle Club. *Studies in Conflict & Terrorism,* 01-29. DOI: 10.1080/1057610X.2018.1455373

Higgins, A. (2018, March 31). *Russia's Feared 'Night Wolves' Bike Gang Came to Bosnia. Bosnia Giggled.* Retrieved from The New York Times: https://www.nytimes.com/2018/03/31/world/europe/balkans-russia-night-wolves-republika-srpska-bosnia.html

Jacoby, T.A. (2016). How the War Was 'One': Countering Violent Extremism and the Social Dimensions of Counter-Terrorism in Canada. *Journal for Deradicalization*, 272-304.

Krupa, D. (2018, August 23). *The Night Wolves, Putin's biker gang*. Retrieved from The Economist : https://www.economist.com/europe/2018/08/23 /the-night-wolves-putins-biker-gang

Lauder, M.A. (2018). 'Wolves of the Russian Spring': An Examination of the Night Wolves as a Proxy for the Russian Government. *Canadian Military Journal, 18*(3), 1-16. Retrieved from http://www.journal.forces.gc.ca/vol18/no3/page5 -eng.asp

Lutsevych, O. (2016). Agents of the Russian World: proxy groups in the contested neighbourhood. *Chatham House.* Retrieved from https://www.chathamhouse.org/sites/files/chath amhouse/publications/research/2016-04-14- agents-russian-world-lutsevych.pdf

Magav2000, director. *7 Мая-День Победы,Мельбурн(Ночные Волки и Русские Мотоциклисты). YouTube*, YouTube, 17 June 2017, www.youtube.com/watch?v=Nqz_NM46rHw.

McCahill, E. (2018, July 20). *Putin's 'Night Wolves' biker gang 'set up European base with armoured vehicles and tanks near small village in Slovakia'.* Retrieved from Mirror : https://www.mirror.co.uk/news/world- news/putins-night-wolves-biker-gang-12952806

McLaughlin, D. (2018, 03 20). *Putin's bikers on Balkan tour as Russia seeks to boost regional influence.* Retrieved from The Irish Times: https://www.irishtimes.com/news/world/europe/putin-s-bikers-on-balkan-tour-as-russia-seeks-to-boost-regional-influence-1.3434024

Night Wolves Motorcycle Club . (n.d.). Retrieved from http://www.nightwolves.ru/nw/

Мотоклуб "Ночные волки", director. *Ночные Волки Прибыли в Австралию Для Участия в Мотоэкспедиции "Православная Австралия 2017". YouTube*, YouTube, 7 Feb. 2017, www.youtube.com/watch?v=qg4emmpsHHg.

Peter, L. (2018, July 31). *Slovakia alarmed by pro-Putin Night Wolves bikers' base* . Retrieved from BBC News: https://www.bbc.com/news/world-europe-45019133

Peter, L. (2018, July 31). Slovakia alarmed by pro-Putin Night Wolves bikers' base. *BBC News*. Retrieved from https://www.bbc.com/news/world-europe-45019133

Read, C. (2018 , August 9). *Putin's 'Night Wolves' biker gang takes over army base in EU sparking World War 3 fears.* Retrieved from Express UK: https://www.express.co.uk/news/world/1000605/russia-news-vladimir-putin-night-wolves-army-base-slovakia-world-war-3

RuptlyTV, director. *Russia: Epic Night Wolves Biker Rally Takes War in Ukraine to the Stage. YouTube*, YouTube, 10 Aug. 2014, www.youtube.com/watch?annotation_id=annotation_324237915&feature=iv&src_vid=h9zjsPxbzNU&v=gu7L4C4xUgQ.

RuptlyTV, director. *Russia: Putin Meets with Night Wolves Biker Club Leader. YouTube*, YouTube, 18 Aug. 2017, www.youtube.com/watch?v=p6lAmB-yEtc.

RuptlyTV, director. *Ukraine: Russian Night Wolves Biker Gang Rolls into Simferopol. YouTube*, YouTube, 28 Feb. 2014, www.youtube.com/watch?v=uPlqYqNWKhk.

Sof1kRedCat, director. *Сергей Комар. Обращение к Братьям. YouTube*, YouTube, 8 Apr. 2015, www.youtube.com/watch?v=LvGDUWpxDNs.

Sputnik. (2015, Septmeber 05). *Russia's Night Wolves Wrap Up Epic WWII Victory Ride to Berlin*. Retrieved from Sputnik International : https://sputniknews.com/europe/201505091021920453/

Sz Planet, director. *Russian Nights Wolves in Australia. YouTube*, YouTube, 6 Mar. 2017, www.youtube.com/watch?v=s7dVH6dxWpQ.

Tabor, D. (2015, October 8). Putin's Angels: Inside Russia's Most Infamous Motorcycle Club. *Rolling Stone*.

Retrieved from
https://www.rollingstone.com/culture/culture-
news/putins-angels-inside-russias-most-infamous-
motorcycle-club-56360/

Telegraf. (2018, March 28). *0 Next time we are going to
Kosovo: Night Wolves revealed where the Russian
influence is felt the most in Serbia (PHOTO)*.
Retrieved from Telegraf Russia:
http://www.telegraf.rs/english/2946528-next-
time-we-are-going-to-kosovo-night-wolves-
revealed-where-the-russian-influence-is-felt-the-
most-in-serbia-photo

Thranholm, I. (2016, March 18). *Russia's Coolest Christian*.
Retrieved from Russia Insider: https://russia-
insider.com/en/christianity/russias-coolest-
christian/ri13436

TRT World, director. *Are the Night Wolves Putin's
Motorcycle Gang? YouTube*, YouTube, 25 Apr.
2018, www.youtube.com/watch?v=3pHXyGqn9fc.

u/Mladen82. (2018, August). *When everybody is
indifferent, the wolves appear*. Retrieved from
Reddit/Slovakia:
https://www.reddit.com/r/Slovakia/comments/95
b77o/when_everybody_is_indifferent_the_wolves
_appear/

World, S. C. (2014, October 08). *Moscow's Night Wolves
bikers are rebels with a cause*. Retrieved from

South China Morning Post:
https://www.scmp.com/news/world/article/1611
538/moscows-night-wolves-bikers-are-rebels-
cause

Zabyelina, Y. (2017). Russia's Night Wolves Motorcycle
Club: From 1%ers to political activists. *Trends in
Organized Crime,* Trends in Organized Crime.

Chapter 6. Media Pack

Berthiaume, L. (2018). Canadians prepare for mock attack on Latvia as real tensions with Russia flare. *The Canadian Press*. Retrieved from https://www.thespec.com/news-story/8859651-canadians-prepare-for-mock-attack-on-latvia-as-real-tensions-with-russia-flare/

Bolotsky, D. (2017). How NATO Uses "the Russian Scare" to Justify Alliance's Eastward Expansion. Retrieved from https://sputniknews.com/in_depth/201710241058495429-nato-russia-military-expansion/

Chivvis, C.S. (2017). Understanding Russian 'Hybrid Warfare': And What Can Be Done About It. *RAND Corporation*. Retrieved from https://www.rand.org/pubs/testimonies/CT468.html

Cusumano, E., & Corbe, M. (Eds.). (2018). *A Civil-Military Response to Hybrid Threats*. The Hague, The Netherlands.

Deutsche Welle. Poland busts Russian 'hybrid warfare' ring. *Deutsche Welle*. Retrieved from https://www.dw.com/en/poland-busts-russian-hybrid-warfare-ring/a-43831566

Global News. (2018). Canadian troops take part in Latvia invasion drill as Russia tensions flare. *Global News*. Retrieved from https://globalnews.ca/news/4408112/canada-latvia-wargames-nato-russia/

Horvath, R. (2015). The Euromaidan and the crisis of Russian nationalism. *Nationalities Papers*, 43(6), 819-839. DOI: 10.1080/00905992.2015.1050366

Johnson, D. (2017). ZAPAD 2017 and Euro-Atlantic security. *NATO Review Magazine*. Retrieved from https://www.nato.int/docu/review/2017/Also-in-2017/zapad-2017-and-euro-atlantic-security-military-exercise-strategic-russia/EN/index.htm

Justin Ling. (2018). In Latvia, Canadian and Italian forces stand on guard with NATO against Russian expansion. *The Globe and Mail*. Retrieved from https://www.theglobeandmail.com/world/article-in-latvia-nato-forces-stand-on-guard-against-russian-expansion/

Kuzio, T & D'Anieri, P. (2018). The Soviet Origins of Russian Hybrid Warfare. *E-International Relations*. Retrieved from https://www.e-ir.info/2018/06/17/the-soviet-origins-of-russian-hybrid-warfare/

Mälksoo, M. (2018). Countering hybrid warfare as ontological security management: the emerging practices of the EU and NATO. *European Security*, 27(3), 374-392. DOI:10.1080/09662839.2018.1497984

McGuinness, Damien. (2017). How a cyber attack transformed Estonia. *BBC News*. Retrieved from https://www.bbc.com/news/39655415

Mezhevich, N. (2015). Russia and the Baltic States: Some Results and a few Perspectives. *International Relations*, 4-12. DOI: 10.5922/2079-8555-2015-2-1

Russia Today. (2018). 'Our build-up is defensive, Russia's aggressive,' says NATO after Putin's remark – but is that fair?. *Russia Today*. Retrieved from https://www.rt.com/news/436617-nato-russia-military-buildup/

Russia Today. (2018). Russia to hold biggest military drills since Soviet times - Defense Minister. *Russia Today*. Retrieved from https://www.rt.com/news/436428-russia-biggest-military-drills/

References

U.S. Government. (2009, March). A Tradecraft Primer:
Structured Analytic Techniques for Improving
Intelligence Analysis. Retrieved from
https://www.cia.gov/library/center-for-the-study-
ofintelligence/csi-publications/books-
andmonographs/Tradecraft%20Primer-apr09.pdf

About CASIS Vancouver

The mandate of the Canadian Association for Security and Intelligence Studies (CASIS) is to empower and enhance research, discussion, and engagement with issues of national security and intelligence. CASIS achieves its mandate, mission, and objectives by employing three pillars; discussion, dissemination and research.

Discussion is accomplished via our monthly roundtable events, special and joint events, and annual conferences.

Dissemination of original research and expert reports is accomplished via the Journal of Conflict, Intelligence, and Warfare (JICW). CASIS Publications are disseminated to various national agencies and organizations.

Original research that CASIS conducts within the fields of security and intelligence are designed to bring awareness to possible emerging threats to Canada and to further encourage the study of intelligence and security. CASIS Vancouver currently has 2 key research projects; Violent Transnational Social Movements, which encompasses

CASIS Vancouver

research on Right Wing-Extremism, and The National Cyber
Research project.

www.ingramcontent.com/pod-product-compliance
Lightning Source LLC
Chambersburg PA
CBHW070810290326
41931CB00011BB/2182